Rowing Home

poems by

Anna Egan Smucker

Finishing Line Press
Georgetown, Kentucky

Rowing Home

Copyright © 2019 by Anna Egan Smucker
ISBN 978-1-63534-999-3 First Edition
All rights reserved under International and Pan-American Copyright Conventions. No part of this book may be reproduced in any manner whatsoever without written permission from the publisher, except in the case of brief quotations embodied in critical articles and reviews.

ACKNOWLEDGMENTS

I would like to thank the editors and staff of the following anthologies in which these poems first appeared, sometimes in slightly different versions:

A Gathering at the Forks: Fifteen Years of the Hindman Settlement School Appalachian Writers Workshop: "Forcing Spring," "Bitter Herb"
Anthology of Appalachian Writers, Silas House, Volume II: "Gift" renamed "Sacrament"
Riparian, Dos Madres Press, "Cable's Eddy" Forthcoming in 2019
Anthology of Appalachian Writers, Wiley Cash, Volume X: "Fifty-Nine Dead, Five Hundred Bleeding"
Anthology of Appalachian Writers, Karen Zacharias, Volume IX: "Such a Time It Was"
Motif v2: Come What May: "About Apples"
Voices on Unity—Coming Together, Falling Apart: "One World"
Wild Sweet Notes—Fifty Years of West Virginia Poetry: "Twilight Along the Ohio," "Bitter Herb"
Women Speak, Volume 3: "Buck Moon Thunder Moon"

I gratefully acknowledge the editors and staff of these journals:

Afield: "Consider the Lilies"
Hamilton Stone Review, No. 16, Fall 2008 The West Virginia Issue: "About Apples" and an earlier version of "Sacrament" titled "Gift"
Still: The Journal: "Cicada" Summer 2018

Publisher: Leah Maines
Editor: Christen Kincaid
Front Cover Art: Painting by Naomi Lees Maiberg
    www.etsy.com/shop/workingwoman
Author Photo: Sally Egan
Front Cover Design: Judith Rempel Smucker
    rempelsmuckerdesign@gmail.com

Printed in the USA on acid-free paper.
Order online: www.finishinglinepress.com
    also available on amazon.com

Author inquiries and mail orders:
Finishing Line Press
P. O. Box 1626
Georgetown, Kentucky 40324
U. S. A.

Table of Contents

Consider the Lilies 1
About Apples 2
Such a Time It Was 3
Cicada 4
Sacrament 5
Ground In 6
Cable's Eddy 7
Willow Island, April 27, 1978 8
Fifty-Nine Dead, Five Hundred Bleeding 9
Regret 10
Forcing Spring 11
Bitter Herb 13
Lost 14
Genealogy 15
The Immigrant 17
Harry's House 18
Summer Twilight along the Ohio 20
Fall Island 21
Hydrology 22
Vertigo 23
A New Eden 24
Buck Moon, Thunder Moon 25
On the Third Day 27
One World 28
Sanctus 30

In loving memory of
Elizabeth M. Aldridge
1904 - 1969
and
James W. Aldridge
1908 – 1987

With my gratitude to long-time friends and fellow writers
Sandy Vrana and Marc Harshman
who have read and given helpful advice
on these poems and so many others over so
many years.

CONSIDER THE LILIES

Past the mid-point of Lent,
good intentions fallen
onto rocky ground,
my breath clouds
the ice-cold window.
I want the fecundity
of warm earth,
these clenched hands
pried open, light to pierce
this darkness.

Outside, wind whips
the tall grass. The red pine's branches
lift and sway. On its plated
bark, sap has hardened into transparent
beads. Last summer's leaves,
dry and curled, rattle
on the lower limbs
of an oak. I pick up what remains
of an acorn: cap, cup, bowl;
inside, a perfect circle
of brown, an eye
without sight, its seed
the absence that speaks.

Perhaps, by now, it has leapt,
transformed into muscle, bone,
the blood of a liquid-eyed deer;
or maybe it lies hidden
a yard away where, by instinct
or luck, a squirrel will unearth it
after a snowfall yet to come.
Or it will not be found,
but lie dormant, forgotten,
until the day it bursts forth
insistent, green, and holy.

ABOUT APPLES

Suddenly I know a lot about apples,
their chambered star-hearts.
I could talk about the nestled seeds,
brilliant as polished mahogany.
Bitter seeds—
enough cyanide to deter
any who would take and eat.
I know, hell-bent on propagation,
they'll kill to survive.

In a dream of fire I search for water,
loop a hotel's canvas hose,
flat as a serpent,
over my arm,
step into a glass elevator,
soar into the sky, step out
to a treeless landscape,
roads radiating
from the five points of a star—
all of them tempting.
No way of knowing
which one's poison,
which one's sweet.

SUCH A TIME IT WAS
for my brother

Remember that place you loved along the river,
under the rumble of trucks on the Fort Steuben Bridge,
where we took our dog, our headstrong, smelly Bowie
who, lucky for us, loved to fetch, and we'd throw
stick after stick out into the murky water then soap him up
after he'd paddled back, the stick a rakish cigar clenched
in his teeth, and how he drenched us when he shook himself
after dropping his treasure at our feet. Everything smelled
like wet dog and Prell and we were kids, neither of us knowing
anything. This, before the Summer of Love, before Vietnam,
before we grew up and changed; and our dog swam farther
and farther out, going after a log instead of our stick,
and he was swallowing water, trying to bring that log to shore,
and you jumped in, swam out to him and brought him home,
you, a hero; and all of us knowing nothing about medals or dog tags,
how they would come to the houses of our ragged town,
how they would come to rest in boxes holding trifold flags.

CICADA

In a sidewalk crack—
its shell,
a relic from its dark life
its long years
of waiting.

As your eyes close
and trees disrobe,
remember sun, the juice
of a perfect pear, shiver
of first love, stars in water
unruffled, deep.

The rush of rain,
an ocean's
roiling undertow;
the waves you named
for sorrows
and then let go.

Night and the rocking
of your tiny boat,
the *slap, slap* that made
you breathe in light;
the trees, the trees—
their new wet leaves.

SACRAMENT

Impossibly thin, Angie's pizzelles
adorned cut-glass Christmas plates.
Stalks of wheat embossed the center
of the anise-flavored offerings
she pressed on family, neighbors, friends.

Turning eighty, something snapped.
Machine-like she churned them out
until counters, cupboards, overflowed.

In the hot kitchen,
her work, her body
had grown articulate:
Eat. Remember me.

GROUND IN

Far gone into Alzheimer's, he put on
his slippers, folded the newspaper under
his arm, and walked into the woods.

Searchers' flashlights found him near dawn
at the bottom of a cliff; its grooved clay
witness to his struggle to climb back up.

"Impossible to pry the dirt
out of your dad's fingernails,"
the undertaker tells my brother
who tells me, handing it on, like in
the child's game of "Pass the Potato"
no one wanting to be left holding.

We visit the place where he died.
Stack rocks to mark his passing.
My fingers fit the grooves he clawed
in that clay. I try to shape them
into words, passing them on,
or trying to.

CABLE'S EDDY

A hard bend in the Ohio
north of Steubenville, north of
Half Moon. Decades away
in my sleep, I still hear
the towboat's two deep moans,
the captain plowing his barges north
warning boats headed down-
river to let him pass.
Clutching the wheel, gauging the current,
his barges' length, width, tonnage,
he aims it all crossways to the flow,
points head-on for the marker
on the western shore,
trusting the river to turn him round,
push him straight, get him through.

WILLOW ISLAND, APRIL 27, 1978

Like the paring
of an apple,
it coiled off.
Scaffolding
tumbled,
cement
unsettled,
not fixed
not set.

Sons,
brothers—
fifty-one
falling,
falling,
fell.

Inspections
not done.
No lights
warned.
No sirens
blared.

Justice—
missing in action
again.
Just a statue,
bowls overflowing
with rain,
unsettling rain.

A cooling tower under construction at the Pleasants Power Station at Willow Island, West Virginia collapsed on April 27, 1978. Fifty-one construction workers were killed, including five members of one local family.

FIFTY-NINE DEAD, FIVE HUNDRED BLEEDING

It might seem callous
to wonder if he wanted
to see if his gun would work—
do the job it was built
and bought to do.

On this blue-sky October day,
how many others wonder
if their guns might have done
it better. How many others
imagine their names, splayed
across headlines, immortal?

I walk the trail alone, along
the Blackwater River where the shade
of hemlock, oak, maple cools me,
where not even a squirrel's scuffle
breaks the stillness. I want to be
this peace where only the ripe fruit
of the hawthorn is as red as blood.

On October 2, 2017, from his room on the 32nd floor of the Mandalay Bay Resort and Casino in Las Vegas, a gunman mowed down a crowd attending a country music festival. It was the worst mass-shooting committed by an individual in modern U.S. history.

REGRET

Nothing extraordinary will happen.
You'll walk down that darkened road

hear the bare-branched trees *click* in the wind,
and try to remember that winter day,

how her lashes brushed your cheek,
how they caught the icy flakes, briefly,

and you'll want that moment—just that one—
the piercing brightness of it
when everything was possible.

But now, more and more often,
you rummage in vain

for those pictures you'd like
to hold, examine,
rearrange.

FORCING SPRING

In February
you cut branches
of forsythia,
and put them
in sweet water
on the windowsill.
And we woke
to springtime
and April
while the snow
drifted deep outside.

Now,
I am the one
who cuts branches
in winter.
And I
make spring
come early,
too.

When the air
turns soft
and the sun
stronger,
I open
every window
and the moist
earth smell
comes in.

But when the bushes
outside the house
are bent boughs
full bloomed,
I grieve
at their
abundance.

For you
are no more
my branch,
my blossom.

BITTER HERB

It grows again, crowding out the lilies,
though we try to root it out every fall.
Leaves deep green, so dark for early spring.
Chow-chow, your mother's name for it,
your black-garbed mother from the old country.

Tough, bitter weed, leaves shaped like swords,
she laced it with vinegar,
chewed it, spat it out.
Weed that forces its way through my flowers
turns up every spring, sure as sorrow.

LOST

> *"It is incompleteness that haunts us."*
> Shirley Hazzard, *The Great Fire*

Letters
whirled
in the wind.

Words
almost
touched
but never
quite

while we
berated
*the inconstant
moon;*
too in love
with night
to know

how even
in daylight
it was always
whole,
always
there.

Now a file
drawer rusted
shut holds
the pieces
that remain . . .

almost enough
almost right
but never
quite.

GENEALOGY
County Mayo, Ireland

On the road from Knock to Kiltimagh,
before the rock lettered *Bohaun*,
just east of the fairy tree,
climb the low stone wall,
pull aside the hundred-year ivy,
uncover what remains.

Sit on the splintered sill.
Swing your legs inside.
Drop to the dirt floor.

In the damp, the dark, see the wreck
of a straw pallet, cracked plates,
moth-eaten coat, scuffed boots,
a lady's shoes, white-velvet with mildew,
soles worn to nothing.
Bottles everywhere ...
smashed.

* * * * * *

Meg thought herself too good
for the boys of Bohaun.
She let her brother Martin live here
after the Black and Tans stripped him,
tied him to a board,
dunked him head first in the river,
held him . . . held him . . . .
When they knew he'd die before telling,
they cut him loose, fired at him,
thought they'd riddled him through,
but he'd sunk himself deep into the water.

Meg had a gun,
wasn't afraid to use it,
kept him hidden
after he'd run naked
home through the fields.

Martin lived here alone
after she died.
The bottles are his.

A horseshoe once nailed up for luck
rusts on the ground.
The pallet remembers flesh.
Shoes remember feet.
The names . . . the stories . . .
No one rests in peace.

THE IMMIGRANT
In memoriam: Robert Emmet, 1788-1803

She fills the fragile, green
sherry glass with Jameson,
toasts the defiant Robert Emmet
hanging over the sideboard.

His *country has taken
her place among
the nations of the earth,*
while her Danny boys
are many years gone.

She fingers her rosaries,
links broken, beads worn,
and stares at the reflection
in her black-specked mirror.

Freeing the braids
that halo her head,
she takes one step,
two, out of time,
holds Emmet's body
in her arms.

Robert Emmet was an Irish patriot. After leading an unsuccessful rebellion against British rule in 1803 he was captured, tried, and executed for high treason. Before he was sentenced, Emmet delivered his famous speech of how his epitaph should not be written until Ireland governed herself.

HARRY'S HOUSE

Dutch, rich, his family's
mansion dominates the Irish
ghetto of Stewartvillle.
Knowing he'll never cross
its threshold again, he asks you,
old friend, to check on it.
He has no one else.

Its gloom behind the leaded
door, is deeper than the house's dark
bricks, heavier than the maroon curtains,
floured with mold and dust, pulled across
windows, blinds shut tight.
The family could have afforded
a housekeeper, servants,
but grief keeps its own—

remembers a celebration, the first streetcar
rolling its shiny wheels into this end
of town, and a young sister of golden curls,
delft blue eyes, a little girl decked
in white dress, red-sashed is run over,
and the house's drapes never open again.

Upstairs, a room, its yellowed walls filled
with age-warped photos—men clean-shaven,
others muttonchopped, moustached, the work
of Harry's brother who liked men better than women,
Harry's brother who took his cameras and traveled west.

After the parents pass, Harry lives on in the back
room where only the shadows visit. A telegram arrives:
Brother dead. Retrieve body from train.
Next day, on the platform, it's thrown at him,
naked, trussed like a chicken.
Harry quits his Saturday nights downtown.
Generous to religious charities, he fills shoeboxes
with their holy cards and statues that glow in the dark.

A wrecking ball and bulldozer make short work
of his dark-bricked house, not one shadow left
on the new highway's cloverleaf. You think
of the four-leafed ones you've found. Lucky.
You've been so lucky.

SUMMER TWILIGHT ALONG THE OHIO

Behind the house, the iron handle of the pump
hangs, a filigree of rust.
An iridescent beetle shoulders its way
into the heart of Grandmother's perfect rose.
In the pounded dirt floor of the foundry,
Grandfather's shattered finger has turned to dust.
A train slices the town in half.

Barefoot children ride down the hard wheels
of the cannon mounted in the town square.
From the river, with the mist rising,
sounds the lowing of a boat
easing into the bend.

The metal box under his bed is empty.

Across the street at the skating rink, a mirrored globe
hurls rainbows across the spinning floor.

FALL ISLAND

There is more decay than I remember
on this tuft of pine and birch
cold-tethered in Long Lake.

Thick moss covers
trunks of fallen pine.
Broken cylinders of birch
burrow into spongy ground.

I trudge among ferns curled and dusty.
Spider threads brush against my mouth,
tangle in my hair.

A crow's caw splits the silence.

The bad boys, the dark waves,
the wild geese, the rising moon
have stolen my boat away.

Out of the mounds of fallen leaves,
Indian pipes lift their tunes.

HYDROLOGY

Fresh from Botany 101,
you tell me there are places
in the desert, small oases

where cottonwood roots drink
rivers in the sun-seared day.
How in the cool of night

high-limbed channels open,
and the water seeps down again
into the cracked, curled earth:

first a spreading stain,
then spurts, spouts, here, there,
until the rivers fill and flow.

And I remember how milk dripped,
then streamed from my breasts
when you, little girl, woke hollow.

How the wail of a stranger's child
commanded the same surge,
my pressure against it powerless.

The wonder of it—
the thirsting, the holding,
the letting go.

VERTIGO

Lying on the wooden dock,
night opens above me,
its darkness shot through with silver.
Suspended between sea and sky,
restless waters below unmoor me.

As a tether, an anchor,
I summon the star chart.
But what cold comfort—the locator pin,
our position so peripheral.

It is the abrasion of sand
that brings me back,
sand from something here before.
I brush it from my shoulders, thighs,
watch it sift into the water.

Under me, fish glide, languid, silent,
at home in this moving sea,
silvery, circling,
drinking it in.

A NEW EDEN

We have journeyed to a place Father christened
Fruitlands, an old farm where
we will be made
perfect.
We will
eat no meat, drink no milk,
for the animals need their flesh and must
have nourishment for their young. Nor will we
clothe ourselves with cotton, for that is picked
by the hands of slaves that must soon, please God,
be set free.
We will
not wear shoes of leather
for animals need their skin
just as we ourselves. No yoke
will be placed on any beast.
We will
till the soil with our
own hands, planting only what grows up—
wheat, barley, nothing base that grows down
into dirt.
And now a man has joined us
who believes clothes hinder the spirit.
At night, we girls,
we will
take turns peering through a keyhole.
We will.

Fruitlands was Bronson Alcott and other Transcendentalists' Utopian experiment that lasted from June 1843 to early January 1844 near Harvard, Massachusetts.

BUCK MOON, THUNDER MOON

Before mothers handed us stapled stacks
of *Dear Abby* columns about sex,
before zit cream, Kotex, and bras,
before garter belts, nylons, and heels,
delirious with anticipation,
we plunged into

Scout Camp at Torch Lake:
kayaking, canoeing,
stretching bow strings taut,
relays, three-legged races,
and snakebite first-aid.

Coyotes *yipped* in the star-streaked nights
as we raced down the woods-trail,
down to the clearing and its glowing fire-heart.
Four tribes of pubescent girls,
we pounded out the rhythm:
Ah-woonie-koonie-cha-ah-woonie;
Ah-woonie-koonie-cha-ah-woonie.

Sweaty hands beating thighs,
blood-sister pacts made and sealed,
we sat cross-legged in a circle,
our chant fast, faster,
the campfire's sparks
scorching the leaves overhead.

Ah-woonie-koonie-cha-ah-woonie,
we swayed like an undulating snake.
At school, Curtis showed me his weenie.
I'd had nothing to show him. Not yet.
Ah-woonie-koonie-cha-ah-woonie.
Ah-woonie-koonie-cha-ah-woonie.

By week's end, sleep deprived,
we had become creatures not ourselves.
Had there been no adult sentry,
we girls would have stripped,
pretended we were colts bucking,
kicking up our shiny hooves,
devouring the long, green grass,
using muscles we didn't know we had.

ON THE THIRD DAY

Art 150's instructor will not
allow us near the wheel. Instead,
we must make our lump of clay
as malleable and warm as
our own flesh. Molding,
squeezing, pounding, shaping.

For months, I knead, smooth, round
my damp, gray ball, wet earth
sinking into the pores
of my palms. Create, crush, make
again, and again. Waking
from a dream of waves
of clay rising, I can feel
the mountains form
in my hands.

ONE WORLD

On a day of clouds whiter than
transfigured robes, from fifty yards
offshore, I watch the branches
of the great white pine,
lifting, falling in the rising wind.

Survivor on this slipping sand,
roots reaching for rocks, crevices,
anything to serve as anchor
against the pushing shoulders of ice,
the weariness of unrelenting wind.

Tree, piercing heaven,
nursed by this wet world,
branches rising like supplicant arms,
hands open, expectant.

Oh, tree, sighing, singing,
lifting up all that is,
all that ever was:
seed, sapling, tree,
garden, Eden, Virgin,
out of Jesse. . .a rod,
a rood, a rising stem.

Seed, sand, descendants
numberless as stars
flung across the void.
In darkness, constellations
invisible wheel and whirl.
All present this radiant day,
longest of the year.

My boat, lifting, falling
on this breathing water,
I pull for shore.
Below me, a net of light,
an illusory cloister grate,
—nothing separating
this world from the other.

SANCTUS
    after Tomas Tranströmer's *"Kyrie"*

At times my life splits open into light—
like a stream carving a new course
after a hundred-year flood.

Moments of mirage, sand as silver water.
It is like being caught in a riptide, watching
the shoreline recede, and trusting, trusting.

Anna Egan Smucker is the author of eight award-winning books. *No Star Nights*, her memoir about growing up in the steel mill town of Weirton, West Virginia in the 1950s, first published by Knopf, won the International Reading Association Children's Book Award. *Golden Delicious: A Cinderella Apple Story*, about the discovery of the Golden Delicious apple in Clay County, West Virginia, and *Brother Giovanni's Little Reward: How the Pretzel Was Born* were chosen to represent West Virginia at the National Book Festival in Washington, D.C. in the years of their publication. *Fallingwater: The Building of Frank Lloyd Wright's Masterpiece*, a picture book about Frank Lloyd Wright's iconic house, co-authored with Marc Harshman and published in 2017 by Roaring Brook/Macmillan, garnered critical acclaim including starred reviews in Publishers Weekly and Booklist, was a Junior Library Guild Selection, and was named an Amazon Children's Nonfiction Book of the Month.

Recipient of a West Virginia Arts Commission Artist Fellowship Award, Anna's poems have been published in several anthologies and journals. She makes her home in Bridgeport, West Virginia. In addition to writing, she enjoys doing author presentations and conducting writing workshops for schools, libraries, and at conferences. Her website can be found at *www.annasmucker.com*

www.ingramcontent.com/pod-product-compliance
Lightning Source LLC
LaVergne TN
LVHW041508070426
835507LV00012B/1409